God Reveals JESUS *To Me,*

a Devoted Muslim Woman

SHADHONA

Copyright © 2014 by Shadhona

God Reveals Jesus To Me, a Devoted Muslim Woman
by Shadhona

Printed in the United States of America

Edited by Xulon Press

ISBN 9781498413800

All rights reserved solely by the author. The author guarantees all contents are original and do not infringe upon the legal rights of any other person or work. No part of this book may be reproduced in any form without the permission of the author. The views expressed in this book are not necessarily those of the publisher.

Scripture quotations taken from the American Standard Version (ASV)- *public domain*

www.xulonpress.com

ACKNOWLEDGEMENTS

My deepest gratitude and heartfelt thankfulness to pastor Henry Wiebe, my mentor, and spiritual counsellor, for being persistent and not giving up on me in inspiring me to write this book. Thank you for believing in me and having faith in me.

A BIG THANK YOU TO:

Udo Schafer

President Of Plexis LTD.

Without your financial aid and technical help, it would have been impossible for me to even write this book. I am truly blessed for God's provision through you.

Donna DiCarlo

For all the time you spent in organizing and fixing my work and giving me all the help I needed to write my story.

Lynda Klassen,
Co-owner of Lincoln Appliance.

For being a prayer warrior, keeping me in your daily prayers.
For your support and being a faithful and loyal friend.
You are that friend in need, who is a friend, indeed.

Vicky Giles.

For staying true to our friendship, and showing me the LOVE of Christ through the good and bad times.
    Always pausing your busy life at any given time, and being there for me when I needed you the most.

Ailene Albidone
Mitch
Carol Taylor
Elaine Felice
Karlene
Donna &
Louise

Lesley Davonport
&
Pastor Michasel Krause

For your love and support, especially your friendship.

Acknowledgements

KC
(Who is no longer here.)

for teaching me to have courage in difficult times by living in your own experience. I miss you.

Benton

Teaching me to forgive and find strength to love again by your own living example.

INTRODUCTION

Over the years, many friends and others would hear my story of how I became a Born-Again Christian from being a devoted Muslim. They would say to me that I should write a book. I would tell them right away that I didn't have any gift in writing; I am good with my hands when it comes to cooking, playing instruments and playing few sports. I did have a dream of someone else writing my story.

Over the past couple of years when I would visit with pastor Henry Wiebe, my mentor and spiritual counsellor, the first thing that he would say to me was, "So when are you writing a book?"

I would respond and say, "I don't have the gift of writing, besides what would I write? Nothing big or exciting is happening in my life."

He then would say to me, "Not too many people have gone through what you have endured. You should write a book."

Because I have such high respect for him, I finally decided to listen to his advice and contacted few publishing companies. I really got a very positive response from Xulon Press. Mark Batterson, whose book my bible study group was working on, sent me an email through Xulon Press and encouraged me to write. As I was praying about it, I found a real sense of peace that God wants me to share my story with the world. Finally, when I communicated with Mr. Newman from the Xulon Press, he really encouraged me to start writing and he also said that he would pray that God would provide the finances for me. This was my final encouragement to start writing, and the rest is history. I surprised myself, not ever writing a book; how by the grace of God did I actually write a book? I even finished it before the date I had originally set to finish it. Praise God!

To respect the privacy of my family, their names have been changed to imaginary names. In honor of my mom, I used my middle name that she chose for me. It is my prayer that as you read this book, you will be touched by the Holy Spirit and be blessed as you discover that JESUS is REAL. A few scriptures that really came to life during my trials and testing times, and guided me back to His grace and comfort in times of my need are: John 15:7, Jeremiah 29:11, Isaiah 43:1-2, 54:14-15, 55:9, 60:11. Psalm 31, 18, 139, 149, 1 Peter 2:24, and 1 John 5:14.

TABLE OF CONTENTS

Chapter 1	My life in Dhaka Bangladesh	13
Chapter 2	My journey to Canada	17
Chapter 3	Adjusting to Alberta Canada	21
Chapter 4	Culture Shock	25
Chapter 5	I challenged God to speak to me directly and He did	29
Chapter 6	Searching for a home church	33
Chapter 7	My baptism	36
Chapter 8	My first Christmas was a miracle	39
Chapter 9	Jesus gives me my birthday wish	44
Chapter 10	Evangelist David Wilkerson's conference in Copps Collisium	48
Chapter 11	Outreach in L.A California	50
Chapter 12	My memorable day Witnessing	52
Chapter 13	Miracle	56
Chapter 14	Hollywood night	59
Chapter 15	Last day in L.A.	62
Chapter 16	Last day in Hollywood	65
Chapter 17	Riverside California	69
Chapter 18	Dreams, visions and miracles in this Castle	71
Chapter 19	Coming to Ridge way Ontario	76
Chapter 20	Moving to a nearby city	80
Chapter 21	Living in the Valley	83
Chapter 22	Lessons learned from my journey as a Christian	89

Shadhona

CHAPTER 1

My life in Dhaka Bangladesh

I was born in the Islamic faith and was a devoted Muslim since I was sixteen years of age. I did everything my religion required of me—from fasting thirty days to praying five times a day with the ceremonial washing before each prayer. I also visited all the holy places of the holy men and drank of the holy water. Even after following all the rituals and prayers, I often found myself sitting on our veranda back in Dhaka Bangladesh. I sat on the marble stool at night wondering who was behind that beautiful sky so beautifully decorated with all the stars and the bright shiny moon? Who came before Adam and Eve?

I still didn't have this peace inside my heart. My vision of God was that He was sitting up behind that curtain of sky holding a big stick and if I did anything wrong, He was going to punish me. As a Muslim, we lived by the Old Testament—the LAW. I lived in fear of God at all times. We were a very wealthy family and also, my dad was a statesman; he fought for the Muslim nation when it was all India under the British Empire. In 1962 my dad, only forty-three years old, died of a heart attack leaving my mother with eleven children. My mother had no education. We had to teach her how to write her own signature now that she was is in control of all his property. We lived in a ten-bedroom mansion with five acres of land with eleven coconut trees and seven mango trees. Mom had our gardener make a vegetable garden and we also had chicken coop. Mom traded coconuts to the market for rice and lentils and meat and that's how she took care of us.

In the summer, I would wake up in the middle of the night and I often saw the lights on in my mom's bedroom. When I peaked in, I would see her sewing, knitting and preparing our fall and winter clothes. In the winter, she would make our summer clothing. My mom was a very wise woman who had many gifts. She was a very creative gourmet cook, and I got my passion for cooking from her. It was a usual afternoon when we all sit at the veranda for our afternoon tea and roasted peanuts. In a moment everything changed when I saw one of my brothers running frantically toward the house from the main gate of the entrance. We had three entrances to the house. He was screaming as he was running toward the house saying that there are tanks and armies on the street and to quickly get in the house. We laughed because he always played pranks on us. Within minutes, there were armies passing by with tanks and we ran in—next thing I know mom put us all under the bed with sheets in our mouths. She lived through the Second World War, and knew a few safety tips.

I asked her "Why do I have sheets between my teeth?" She said, "Because when the bomb drops, it won't break my teeth." Next thing I knew, I was hearing the loud noise of the bomb and life suddenly changed for me completely. I had to endure this civil war between East and West Pakistan for nine months. We fought the West and won the war of liberation and now the former East Pakistan is called Bangladesh. After this war was over, I finished my high school and then graduated from a two-year diploma from the Music College with major in sitar (a classical instrument) and tabla (percussion). But when I went to apply to the largest music academy in Dhaka for tabla lesson, I was denied simply because I was a woman. Even though I had the foreknowledge of women being treated as second-class citizens and we had no voice, I still was shocked at the rejection I received. So I decided to be persistent until they accepted my application.

I was mocked by the men and also there were no female students in the tabla class and the men made sure to tell me that I was not welcomed. After having many debates with the academy board and even being the guest in a live television show about my passion to learn this male dominated instrument, I finally was accepted into this tabla class (with twelve men in this class and myself). Each of these three years that I took this class at the end of each year the principal would announce, "Shadhona first class first in tabla." This made the men even angrier, and they cut my drums at times and they would also throw stones at my rickshaw when I was on my way to the school. Thank God I had my mom's support. The day before I left for Canada, I was at the university to gather my credits and a few women came up to me and said, "Are you Shadhona?" I said, "Yes." They replied, "Thank you. Because of you, we can now take tabla lesson in the music schools." Wow it made me very happy to be able to be the voice for women. Shortly after I attended the university, mom became very ill with polycystic kidney disease and my brother, who lived in Edmonton Alberta at the time, brought her to Canada for treatment. I had to come against my wishes because in my culture one cannot leave an unmarried daughter if there is no next of kin to take care of her. So I gave up my dreams of getting a PHD in Music and followed my mom and my two siblings to Edmonton Alberta where my oldest sister and my older brother sponsored us to come and live in Canada.

Shadhona

Chapter 2

My journey to Canada

After much pleading to my mom not to take me with her to Canada, I still had to leave my dream behind and pack my bags. We were a well-known family and had many relatives so the airport was full of people who came to say goodbye to us. I was beside myself with tears running down my face and with each step I took toward that big Boeing, I started to panic and still wished mom would have a change of heart—but no such luck. As I approached the plane and started to step on the plane ladder, I looked back and saw so many faces behind the glass; my friends from the University and Music College were all waving their hands. I finally entered the plane and as soon as it took off, I completely broke down and cried out loud. I know that I embarrassed my two siblings and my mom. I think I fell asleep and when I woke up, the plane was in the clouds, and it was a very long flight to Canada. On our way to Canada, mom wanted to stop in Amsterdam and stay there for few days. She wanted to reminisce about her past. Dad used to read a novel to her that had Amsterdam in the story and so she wanted to see with her naked eyes the place she had to only imagine before. So we stayed three days in Amsterdam and visited Copenhagen. After that, we left for Canada and it seemed like the flight took forever.

Our flight with KLM, the largest plane I have ever seen, had four aisles of seats. Finally, after what seemed like a few days in the sky and the passing of many oceans, seas and mountains we arrived in Chicago. After the custom check, we got in a plane that looked and felt like a helicopter compared to this KLM flight I just got off from. So this is the final flight to Canada and as the pilot announced the take-off for Edmonton, I was so tired after the long custom check that I closed my eyes and drifted off to sleep as I was thinking of all the friends I left behind in Bangladesh. When I woke up, the steward gave me a hot towel and told me that we would be landing shortly. A few minutes later, the captain announced the landing, so I put my seat-belt on and with a loud noise, the plane came to a landing and slowly came to a halt by the gate where we were to get off. I couldn't see my sister Salena and as we got off the plane, we had to go through customs again. I was whispering under my breath, *Oh lord don't let it be that long again.*

After maybe an hour, the door was opened and as we walked out of customs, we saw Salena. She looked so tiny and she is my big sister, the oldest of all four sisters. We hugged and then she took us to the baggage claim and after we got all of our many suitcases, we got into her car. I was amazed to see her drive as I never saw a woman drive before. The ride was so quiet because no one was blowing their horns for the cows or goats to get off the road and this was deafening to my ears.

I finally asked my sister "Is there a curfew or something? Where is everybody? The road is so empty with no noise is there a civil war going on?" She laughed and said, "No nothing is wrong. This is Canada. Welcome to Edmonton, people don't honk here; they follow the traffic rules." I know that it was August and summer in Edmonton, but I was so cold in my sari. It was the 13th of August, three in the afternoon when we came to Edmonton, and as I was looking out the window of her car, I saw a few cars quietly pass us by. Now when we arrived at my brother's house, it was a very big two storied house down by the river. My sister Salena, who bought all our furniture and wardrobes, was so excited to show me and my younger sister, Pramela and brother Nahun, our bedrooms. Everything looked so beautiful I thanked my sister profusely and hugged her and I went to my room. I felt like I was deaf because I just couldn't seem to get over how silent it was here. My sister took me shopping for clothes. This was apparently one of the hottest days in Edmonton, but this is what I wore to the store. God bless my sister for staying with me. I wore leotards under my jeans, a turtleneck under my denim shirt and then a parka and mittens. When we arrived at the mall, I noticed that all the women and girls were wearing halter tops and shorts and I was still so cold and asked if I could get some hot chocolate. People outside the mall were staring at me; I think they were thinking that they we were the only ones with igloos.

Shortly after, I started to feel very lonely and depressed. I didn't know how to speak English and I remember going to a store and pointing at the milk to let them know what I wanted. That's the day I decided to teach myself how to speak English. I watched TV and tried to learn from the people's expressions what they were saying and I memorized words that I would hear others say. I never ever saw any couple in my country show any type of affection toward one another let alone kiss. As I walked down the street to catch a bus, I noticed that people were so open in their affection and young men and women kissed so openly that I would just look away. That's private in my culture so I was amazed and as I looked away, there were times when I would hit a lamp post. I was accepted at the University of Alberta but for the fear of not being able to speak fluent English, I didn't attend. This is one of my biggest regrets. Instead, I went to a community college and took photography and journalism for one semester and worked at a high-end restaurant called "Blackbeard".

Shadhona

CHAPTER 3

Adjusting to Alberta Canada

It was very cold for someone like me who was from a country that had no winter and to be faced with such severe weather. Where I came from, people were very friendly to one another on the streets, so I was trying to be friendly to the people at the bus stop while waiting for the bus. Very often, I got a serious look back or they would ask me "Do I know you?" I would say "No, just thought of being friendly." As the winter weather continued, I realized why people don't want to smile. First of all, their mouths are covered with their winter scarves, and I also realized when I tried to smile my teeth would really hurt. I was afraid to lose my teeth so I stopped smiling too before the winter really got colder. On my first day of work, I was very alone because I didn't know anyone. It seemed that during the coffee break, people would often sit at the table where everyone knew each other and I felt left out. Not only did I feel left out but I also felt awkward listening to other conversations at the table. So, I finally decided to sit at a table by myself and mind my own business. In the summer of 1979, I was having my usual coffee break sitting at a table by myself and a young woman came to my table and asked if she could sit with me. I replied, "Sure." She sat down and smiled and introduced herself saying, "Hi my name is Janice. I'm a university student and this is my summer job."

I replied, "My name is Shadhona." She was a tall thin blonde with a beautiful smile. I was pleasantly surprised that someone actually came to my table and was so friendly enough to sit with me through my break. When I went to my department, which was 'filing', I noticed Janice also worked in this department. As the days and weeks went by, Janice continued to sit with me during my coffee break now and even during my lunch break. Soon we became more than co-workers and we became acquaintances. Just before summer was over, Janice and I became friends and we exchanged phone numbers so we would keep in touch. Just a few months before while having lunch, she started to share her faith with me and explained that she was a born again Christian. I had no idea what that meant, but I didn't bother to know anything further because I was devoted and loyal to my religion "Islam". Besides, the only knowledge I had from my childhood were the Christians who lived at our rental house. They would party all night Saturday, get drunk and then go to Church on Sunday and they called themselves "Catholics".

At the end of summer, Janice left for school and I continued on with my work. To my surprise one day, I got a call from Janice and she invited me for dinner. So, I went and had a great time and after supper as we were talking, she started to talk about her faith again. I said, "Janice I am a devoted Muslim, have been all my life, there is only ONE HOLY GOD and no other God and prophet Mohammad is his prophet."

She smiled and just wanted to discuss more about what I believed and was trying to witness to me about Jesus Christ. At that moment, I decided to end the evening and went home. I said to myself on my way home, "I wondered if this is why she invited me to dinner so she could talk about her God." Soon Janice and I became close friends. I liked spending my coffee break and lunchtime with her, even though I didn't like her mentioning Christianity. At least she didn't use bad language or smoke when I was with her like the other co-workers. It was a beautiful summer day, so I thought of sitting outside and have a donair. As I was sitting under my favorite tree, Janice came and joined me for lunch. Today, instead of talking about her faith, she surprised me by asking me what I believed and asked about Islam. So I shared with her that the Islamic religion believes in One Holy God and His prophet Mohammad. We fast for thirty days during Ramadhan; we eat before sunrise and break our fast after the sunset. Then after thirty days are over, we rise up early to pray. Thousands of men go out in an open field and pray and when the prayer is over we have a feast, desserts snacks and special meals like *biriyani.* This is a very fancy dish that has basmati rice with saffron, and goat meat or lamb and potatoes and it's all cooked in layers. Then we also do the ritual of Abraham sacrificing his son in faith and God (Allah) turned his son into a lamb, so our next holiday is called "*Eidul Zoha*" where we sacrifice a goat, cow or lamb in front of our house and ask God to forgive all our sins. Janice appeared very curious and interested and asked how many times we pray because she heard that we prayed a lot. I replied, "We pray five times a day with a ceremonial wash each time. I told her that when

I turned sixteen I decided to follow my Islam faith and to devote myself to my religion." I told her, "There are scriptures from the Quran, which is our Holy book all over the place in our house. It's above the door post; it's on your floor mat; it's on most mens' forehead or wrist inside a brass bracelet. The reverential fear of God is very loud in my culture. Islam is a religion, ethnicity, and a culture."

    Janice replied "Wow sounds like your religion seems to have lot of laws and do's and don'ts. I said, "Quran mostly consists of the Old Testament; we call God the God of Abraham and Moses. Ten Commandments is the law we live by."

Shadhona

CHAPTER 4

"Culture Shock"

    I have been in Edmonton now for two years and I still am getting used to the climate, culture and still learning the language. I am finding all of this overwhelming. One day one of my co-workers Cori asked, "Hey Shadhona how are you adjusting to our weather and culture?"

I replied with a sigh, "I am finding the language very complicated and the weather very exhausting to my body I am not use to this kind of cold weather." And I told her, "And to answer your question about the culture, I really had a culture shock when I first came here. I found out that the white people don't like the dark skinned people like me." I was so shocked. People don't like me simply because I have dark skin? Then after the shock came my confusion when I witnessed white men and mostly women laying out in the sun, half-naked in the summer trying to get dark like me."

They all laughed when I said that and said, "It is funny, but we don't all dislike dark skinned people." In my culture men and women are not allowed to date. We have arranged marriages; your parents decide whom you are going to marry. The parents of a man when they think he is ready to marry will go out and look for a suitable bride for him. They literally check the women like they check chicken or goat. They check to see if she has enough meat on her—not too skinny—they check her teeth to make sure she has all her teeth and they are real teeth and also watch her as she walks to see that she is not walking crooked or limping while she walks. When I was attending the Dhaka University, I noticed when I would come home that there were a few women talking to mom about their son and wishing to choose one of mom's daughters as a suitable bride for him. Soon I realized they were talking about choosing me. One day I came home early and found my pictures on the coffee table and these women were looking at them and mom was sitting with them smiling at me. I got scared that this meant that my dream of getting a Ph. D in music was over and I would have to become a total stranger's wife for the rest of my life. I couldn't let that happen so I came up with a solution. I went to the kitchen and asked my servant to take her old ripped sari and to take my silk expensive sari. She was afraid to lose her job if she did that so I assured her that I would make sure she had her job. So after wearing her sari, I walked across the living room where these ladies were sitting and walked by as crooked as I could be and also walked with a limp. When I went in my room and turned around, mom was right there because she followed right behind me. She slapped me and I looked at her and said "thank you mom for this slap, I would rather endure your slap then to be sold to a strange man." The next

"Culture Shock"

day, to make sure I was safe from another bargain, I put up a sign on my door that read THIS CHICKEN IS NOT FOR SALE. My co-workers had a good laugh after they heard my story. When I came to Canada, I noticed that men and women openly socialized with each other. I remember the first time a guy asked me out and I didn't understand what he was asking. In my culture the word DATE means two things; one is a fruit and the other is the calendar but I soon learned what it meant. It is summer of 1980 and Janice came back to work at worker's compensation and in the filing department where I worked. I was really happy to see her because I didn't really keep in touch with her through her school years. One Friday she invited me to her church to watch a movie about Jesus Christ and I went because I hadn't seen her for a while. It was about the crucifixion of Jesus. After the movie, she asked me what I thought of the movie and I replied, "I hate looking at blood and if Jesus's enemies wanted him dead why didn't they simply take a gun and shoot him? Why did they make him suffer for three days?" She didn't say anything to my statement and we just went for coffee and I came home and had a hard time sleeping that night because of all the blood I saw in the movie.

    Often I would be approached by different people when I got off the bus on my way to work or coming home. One group called themselves "Jehovah Witness" and the other people would be in black suits and have this cracked coconut smile on their faces (they called themselves "Mormons"). With these people trying to convert me to their religion including Janice, didn't convinced me to follow their faith. For me, it was like 2 +2 should equal 4, but instead it equaled 5. It confused me about their beliefs and it frustrated me because nothing made sense. So every time I ran into one of these people, I ran the other way, especially the Jehovah's because I thought they were too aggressive and pushy in their approach. I finally told Janice that if we were going to be friends, I would appreciate it if she didn't talk about her Jesus every time we were together, and she agreed. I noticed people I worked with didn't really associate with Janice and they would gossip about how she was weird and nerdy. I was her only friend, at least at work. I would often think of what Janice shared with me privately when I was alone. One thing I know bothered me the most was when Janice talked about her God. It felt like she was so close to God and I know my vision of God as a Muslim was that He was way up in the sky with a long beard and holding a stick and as soon as I did anything wrong, He would punish me. I would have to earn His approval and affection by good merit with the "Do's and "Don'ts". To me, Janice always appeared to have peace from within and was always joyful and happy. I wondered what her secret was to be this peaceful and she was so different from other people around me. It was the end of August and I knew this was Janice's last month at work and soon she would go back to school so one evening, I invited her for dinner. She loved my food and I told her music and cooking were my two passions. I loved to cook gourmet. That night Janice shared more about Jesus and this time I didn't mind because I knew this was probably the last time I would see her until next year. I asked her what her secret was of having this calmness about her and being so peaceful. She smiled and told me Jesus was the reason for her peace and joy and before she left that night, she gave me a gift. I opened it and it was a Bible that read "American Standard Bible". I didn't want to offend her so I accepted it knowing that I would throw it out on garbage day.

Shadhona

Chapter 5

I challenged God to speak to me directly and He did

*I*t was Friday. I was always happy to get off work on Friday because it meant that the weekend was here and I could sleep in. My co-workers usually invited me out for drinks but I don't drink so I declined their invitation. I came home and did my usual thing. I went jogging then came home and made myself dinner then stayed up late, watched a movie then went to bed. I made sure the alarm was off. Saturday is usually a cleaning day and laundry day. Sunday, I sometimes met my sister and we usually went for lunch for Chinese food or a sub, and I did meet her that Sunday. After I came home, I watched TV and as I was turning the channels, I came to a Christian program. I was listening to this man claiming that Jesus healed his knee and the audience was clapping with excitement. I sat in front of the TV and laughed, and said out loud, "Here we go more mumbo jumbo." I was bombarded by people telling me about their God, so I changed the channel to a better show. That night, as I was getting ready for bed, I looked in my mirror in the bathroom and said out loud "God if Jesus is really up there and He is real then why don't you speak to me directly. All these people telling me about Jesus is not making sense to me 2+2 is not adding to 4. I tell you what, if you speak to me directly not only will I believe in Jesus, I will also serve you the rest of my life." Then I went to bed, it was the last Sunday of August 1980.

In the middle of the night, I was awoken by what felt like someone entering my bedroom. I looked around and said, "Who is there?" but there was no answer so I turned around and went back to bed. A few minutes later, I again felt someone's presence in my room so I got up and turned the light but I saw no one. I thought this was weird. Then I smiled and said to myself, "Oh, because Janice and others talk to me about Jesus, I'm having a psychological moment and I am too smart to fall for this". I rolled back to bed, looked at the clock and it was 2:00 in the morning so now I'm really trying to sleep. A few minutes later, I felt the same thing again, only this time it felt like someone actually sat on my bedside, and I actually felt the bed bounce a bit. I instantly jumped out of the bed and turned the light on but no one was in the room but I immediately heard a voice inside my head—not out loud say, "Go read my word and know who Jesus is." Suddenly I remembered challenging God to speak to me directly and I fell down on my knees and cried out to God. I said, "God please don't take my life. I am sorry. Please forgive all my sins and I accept Jesus into my heart. Please God don't take my life."

For the first time, I felt such a peace in my heart. I used to laugh when I saw on television how Christians proclaimed the peace they have because Jesus came into their life. I now realized how true and real this feeling is. Then I went to my utility closet and took out the bible that Janice had given me and the one I was going to throw out the next garbage day. I went into to my bedroom and opened it and it fell on Gospel of John Chapter 3, where Jesus was speaking to Nichodimus about how to be born again. After reading this chapter, I was still on my knees when all of a sudden it hit me like a thunder and I said to myself, "I am in the presence of the Almighty Holy God and He just spoke to me". I was at awe and speechless. I finally went to bed, but couldn't sleep after this encounter with God, as I was pondering on what just took place; I slowly drifted off to sleep. I woke up the next morning with strong feelings about what happened the night before. As I got ready for work, I made sure I took the Bible with me. I was reading the Bible and was so excited to get to know Jesus. The man who was sitting next to me looked at me, and with a shocked look on his face he said to me, "Are you really reading the Bible in public?"

I replied, "Why not? You are reading your book and I am reading mine what's the difference?" He smiled and said, "Usually people are very private about their beliefs and faith and I have never seen anyone be so open about his or her faith or read their Bible so publicly." I told him that I wasn't ashamed of my faith or Jesus. I also explained that I worked full time so first thing in the morning while my mind was still fresh I liked to use my time on the bus to read my Bible and to get to know Jesus. I had already called Janice to give her the good news so when she saw me at work, she gave me a big hug. I still remember when I called her and shared with her how God spoke to me. On other end of the phone, I could hear her shouting out, "Praise the Lord" and laughing with joy. As soon as my co-worker saw me she asked me why I was so happy that day so told her that I became a Born Again Christian. She just laughed and told me few crude jokes about Jesus so I simply ignored her. Later in the day, as I was filing the files in the cabinet, Cori and few other co-workers were continuing to make fun of my experience of becoming a Christian and were still saying jokes about Jesus. My supervisor came out of her office and said to me, "Doesn't it bother you how they are making fun of you and laughing at you? How can you stay so calm and not let it bother you?" I told her that I had such a joy in my heart it was not bothering me. Besides, I knew that they would love for me to react and I didn't want to give them the satisfaction so my boss laughed and went back to her office.

Shadhona

Chapter 6

Searching for a home church

My first Sunday morning as a new Born Again Christian and I was thinking "what now?" I know I need to attend church but where? Which church do I go to? So after breakfast I opened up the yellow pages and started looking for a church that I could go to. Wow, the list for churches seemed almost as long if not longer as the restaurant pages. I thought to myself that it was easier to enter the kingdom of heaven as there is only one heaven, but to choose a church, now this is going to be tough. I know that Janice invited me to attend her church, but I didn't want to be influenced by any one as to which church I wanted to attend. So I started calling all the different denominational churches and asked questions about their churches. As many as I called, they were all very accommodating in sharing the doctrine of their denomination. I went to a catholic church and talked to a nun and after I shared my encounter with God and how I came to accept Jesus as my Savior, I will never forget what she said to me. She said, "O child I have been a nun for fifty years and as I was listening to your testimony I had shivers down my back. Don't come to this church, go find another church". So I started my hunt again for a church and I remember talking to a pastor from a Brethren church. I was a bit upset, coming from a culture where women are treated with less freedom and respect so I took it a bit personally that there were no sistern in the church. So I asked the pastor, "How come you don't have any sistern in your church?" The pastor laughed and said "women and men attend here" and explained to me what the term "Brethren" meant and also educated me in what the word "sistern" meant here with the spelling "Cistern". I then called my boss from Husky's Restaurant where I worked for the summers and who I kept in touch with over the years. After she found out that I became a Christian and was now looking for a church, she invited me to her church. She was a Mormon and so I went to her church but after listening to the pastor for what seemed like forever, I leaned over to my boss and whispered, "When do you take coffee break?" With a smile she whispered back, "Mormons don't drink coffee."

I replied, "Are you kidding me? No coffee when is this going to end?" And she said, "In a short while." It was almost two hours when the service finally ended. I was so hungry to hear about Jesus in this service, but I didn't hear much about my Savior and so I was very disappointed. One Sunday, I decided to go to the Penticostal Tabernacle Church not far from where I lived. This is where Janice and her sister Nadine went. I had an instant connection with the pastor the moment we shook hands. He was praising God when he heard how God spoke to me and I came to accept Jesus. I asked him about the vision I saw right after I accepted

Christ in my bedroom while still on my knees. I said the vision of His face and His cheek looked so muddy. Pastor James McKnight replied with a big smile on his face and said to me, "You know in scripture it mentions of how they plucked His beard and that would make sense that you saw His cheek muddy with a blood clot." Central Tabernacle is a very big church with a congregation of about three thousand people. Here, if I ever had any questions about the Bible, and trust me I had many questions, I would call the church and no matter how busy he was, he always took my call and answered all my questions. Sometimes I would make a gourmet lunch and share a bit of my culture and food with him in his office and he would share his wisdom and knowledge of God and the Bible with me. What a blessing that God would bring Pastor Mcknight into my path to mentor, lead and guide me to grow spiritually stronger. I was always amazed how much compassion pastor Mcknight and his lovely family showed me when I was attending the church.

Shadhona

Chapter 7

My baptism

It's now October and this month is a month of caution for our family. As long as I can remember, something bad always occurred in October. I remember my sister would make a special phone call to me when October would arrive and she would say "It's October and you know the unfortunate things that happen to our family in this month, so be careful, especially on the twentieth of the month." One October on the twentieth my dad passed away, the next year in the same month and date, my uncle died. The next October on the same date, my brother fell under a moving bus and almost died. So when I heard that my church was having a baptism service on October twentieth, I thought twice about whether I should get baptised. I was really struggling emotionally; this has been a tradition in our family to be cautious. I didn't want anything bad to happen when I got baptised. After praying about it, I decided that by His Grace I will get baptised with a positive attitude,

My baptism

and turn this gloomy month into a joyful month, and from here on, when October comes I can think of something wonderful that happened in my life, I got baptised. So I decided to get baptised on the 20th of October. This is now two months after I became a born again Christian. I decided to fast for three days, and started on Friday and decided to break my fasting after I got baptised on Sunday the 20th of October. I prayed and asked Jesus for two things before Sunday came; I asked that He would take away my desire for McDonald's for these three days , and I wanted something special from Him. I prayed that He would stretch my height an inch longer than I am now which was five feet tall. I felt no craving for McDonald's food for these three days and when Sunday came I was so excited that I couldn't wait for the evening baptism service. It was now 6pm and I was already at church in a room with others who were also getting baptised. They gave us instructions about how it was going to take place, and where we were to go after we got baptised. I already had my teaching about what baptism was about, from pastor Mcknight. He explained that it was a ritual that symbolizes Christ's death and resurrection. So when I get emerged under the water it is a symbol that I died with Him and when I come up again it is the symbol that I have also risen with Him. When the service started, I was anxiously waiting for one of the elders to call my name, and next thing I heard was my name and I was so excited that pastor Mcknight was baptising me. I went in the big warm water tub and he asked me in a few words to share with the congregation my testimony. So I did this and then I held my breath and was also holding my nose when he emerged my body gently under the water and brought me back again. I was soaking wet and all I could hear were the people clapping their hands. Right after I got baptised,

I was very hungry so I went to McDonald's and had my favorite McChicken sandwich.

The next morning, when I was getting ready for work, I felt like I was so tall that my head was almost touching the ceiling. Now I know that I wasn't really that tall, but it was this feeling I couldn't shake off. When I went in front of my dresser as I always did, to brush my hair, I noticed that my head was a bit above the mirror. All of a sudden I remembered that I asked Jesus for something tangible from Him; an inch of growth to my height. I right away called the nurse at work and asked her to please check my height on my file. She did and said, "You are five feet tall. Why?" I told her that I was coming to work early to take my measurement again. After I got off the bus, I literally ran the rest of the way to work and went up to her office. I was out of breath when I got there, and asked her, "Please Nancy take my height again." She brought me to the measuring stick and told me to stand still. I did. I impatiently asked, "So what is my height?" She replied, "Well you were 5 feet before but now you are 5 feet 1 inches tall."

With a big smile on my face I repeated, "Yes, He did it. He gave me what I asked for." Then I shared with her what I asked of Jesus before I got baptised and how He answered my prayer. She didn't say anything, but her face was very still and in shock.

Shadhona

Chapter 8

My first Christmas was a miracle

It's December, and I was thinking this would be my first Christmas to celebrate as a new Christian. Today when I went to work I asked Janice "what do you do at Christmas as I have never celebrated this holiday before?" She explained that it was the birthday of our Lord Jesus and that's the main thing and there's usually a very special service at church on the 24th, Christmas Eve. We have a feast with family and friends. We cook lots of food—turkey is the centrepiece for the dinner and all kinds of goodies. We also exchange gifts with our siblings and our parents and they also give us gifts they are wrapped nicely in decorative wrapping papers and we put them under the tree. I was excited when she mentioned gifts. I love that. I love to give gifts to my friends. Then I asked again, "Where does Santa fit in? What's the connection between Santa and Jesus?" She laughed and replied "Santa has nothing to do with Jesus. Santa is an imaginary person who comes on Christmas

Eve down through the chimney and leaves gifts for kids who have been good throughout the year. This whole thing about Santa has been created for kids". I replied, "so this Santa thing is a traditional part of Chrismas?" Now I understand that the tradition of Christmas has nothing to do with the essence of Christmas. Janice smiled and said, "You got it."

During the last two weeks of December, I started to get excited about Christmas because it was Jesus's birthday. I would come home from work and after supper, did some cleaning around the house as I wanted my apartment to be spic and span clean on His birthday. The last week before the holiday, I was taking some files on the fourth floor and as I got into the elevator, my friend Connie got in the elevator with me. As we were chatting, she asked "So Shadhona what are you doing for Christmas?" I said to her, "I am alone and I know this is Jesus's birthday so I will celebrate His birthday by going to the Christmas Eve service and then light some candles at my place and make my special meal that we made back in Bangladesh during our holidays called *biriyani*." Connie was impressed. Then she looked again and said, "Would you like a Christmas tree? Every year my family goes out in the country to get a real tree." I was so excited so I took her up on her offer and she brought me the Christmas tree that evening. I was still washing my windows and singing "Joy to the World", and I was telling Jesus, "I am just excited that it is Your birthday I don't need anything else to make me happy." The next day, I saw Connie and she asked if I liked my tree and I said, "Yes I put it in a bucket with water as it's a plant right?" Connie laughed and said, "You need a stand for it and actually I have an extra one so I'll bring it tomorrow." I thanked her, but under my breath was wondering what a stand was and how do I assemble it?

She gave me the stand the next day and after I came home, I was looking at it with no clue about what to do with it. My neighbour, who often came over for sugar or some spice, knocked on my door and asked if he could borrow some sugar. I let him in and as I went to the kitchen, he asked me if I knew how to put the tree up. I told him that I had never had a Christmas tree in my whole life so I had no idea how to put it up. He immediately offered to put up my tree with the stand under it and I was so relieved and thankful. I went back to my cleaning and sang, "Joy to the World." It was Friday, the last day before Christmas and I arrived home. I was looking at the tree thinking what do I do now? Next thing my phone rings, and it's my older sister Salena who says, "Shadhona, usually my husband and I celebrate Christmas here, but this year Tim and I are going to visit his parents in Vancouver, so I was wondering if you have a tree and if you need decorations, you can have my decorations."

I almost in disbelief shouted out, "Yes, yes I would love to." She came over that night and dropped off the decorations, and complimented my tree. After she left, I opened the big box and saw mini lights and ornaments. I stared at them and was so lost as to what to do, but I started singing "Happy Birthday" to Jesus. A little later that night, my sister called again and almost in panic she said, "Did you already decorate the tree?" I told her that I had no idea what to do or how to decorate and that I was just sitting there completely lost.

She was relieved that I didn't and said, "Thank God, Pramela, who is my younger sister, always decorated my tree over the year as a tradition; now she is all upset this year she won't be able to because we are not going to be here, can she come and decorate the tree? It would make her so happy."

I was so excited and I replied, "Absolutely she is more than welcome to come and decorate. Tell her to come tonight if she wants to." A few hours later, Pramela was at my door and I welcomed her in. She decorated my tree so beautifully and I knew that I could not have done that on my own. After she decorated the tree, she left. Saturday morning I was so excited that this was the weekend that I got to celebrate Jesus's birthday and that's all that mattered to me. After I washed the windows and did the rest of the cleaning, I turned the Christmas tree on and it looked so pretty. As I was sitting in my living room and enjoying the tree, there was a knock on my door. I couldn't believe my eyes when I opened the door and saw my sister Salena standing there holding gifts wrapped in shiny paper. I let her in, they were all for me. I counted, there were fourteen gifts just for me. Wow!

She put them under my tree and said, "Now the tree is complete." Then she said, "I know I won't be here for Christmas, but since the tree is all decorated here why don't we have Christmas dinner here? You, Pramela, me and Tim. What do you think?" I replied, "Yes, but what should I cook?"

She laughed and said, "Don't worry I will make the turkey and all the trimmings and bring it here." I couldn't believe how everything was falling in place for me, starting with Connie giving me the tree, my neighbour putting it up for me, Salena giving me all the decorations and Pramela decorating the tree and now all the gifts she brought and put it under the tree. What a miracle! This is truly a Christmas Miracle that the Lord blessed me with. So Sunday evening, Salena brought the full course turkey dinner and as we sat around my new clean table, I was surprised when Salena looked at me and asked if I would say grace for the meal and I was more than happy to do so. After dinner we opened gifts and there were so many gifts my sisters gave me I felt like a kid. I was just happy that this was Jesus's birthday that's all I needed to celebrate Christmas, but the Lord added all these for me out of the goodness of His heart. A Bible verse came to me when I went to bed that night "Seek ye the Kingdom first and all these things shall be added unto you." (Matthew 6:33)

Shadhona

CHAPTER 9

Jesus gives me my birthday wish

I still remember this winter morning in 1981 around early spring. After my devotion, I asked Jesus that I would like to have something special from Him for my birthday. I heard a voice in my head saying, "Read Psalm 139." With excitement I opened up my bible and looked for psalm 139, but I couldn't find it. With much disappointment, I called Janice and shared my disappointment. I told her," I really thought He spoke to me but there is no psalm 139 in the Bible." Janice asked, "What did you look under?" I replied" I looked under saam."I still wasn't really familiar with the bible. Janice said to me "look under Psalm." I thanked her ended the phone call went to my Bible and actually found psalm 139. Wow! Jesus did give me by birthday wish, I couldn't believe my eyes as I was reading. It described my birth and how God knew me before I was even formed in my mother's womb. This psalm is all about birth, praise the Lord.

A few weeks later one Sunday morning, I was making a melody to a song I wrote. Shortly after I became a follower of Jesus, I bought a guitar and taught myself how to play a few chords and started writing songs to worship Him through music. I am a musician, a percussionist and I also play Sitar and different kinds of percussion. Music is a big part of my life; it ministers to me deeply. So, as I was in bed and trying to come up with a melody for the lyrics of my song, I heard a voice in my head again saying, "Go read Psalm 149." This time I know how to look up a psalm, got excited again got out of bed and opened by Bible and found psalm 149. I read and with astonishment couldn't help but come to a halt in verse 5. This is what the verse says, "Let the godly ones exult in glory, let them sing for joy on their beds."

That's exactly what I was doing in my bed. I thought to myself, "This is so cool, Jesus is really REAL. He actually talks to me wow. I feel so blessed. I couldn't wait to go to church that morning and share this unique experience with my friends. When I got there a few of my friends were waiting to sit with me and I right away with great joy, shared with them what took place that morning. They were so happy for me and were praising the Lord with me. Someone once asked me, "How do I know that God is speaking to me?"

I said to her, "If God is speaking to you He will always confirm it, either through scripture or through someone else." Shortly after the service started this morning, our choir director came to the podium and opened the Bible and read the scripture for the day, and as he was reading it I had shivers and could barely contain my joy and excitement because he read psalm 149 and stopped at verse 5. There is my confirmation, I almost fainted, once again, to realize that Jesus is so REAL. The next day at work, Cori asked me to pray for her so that God would heal her swollen cheek and her teeth. She had a sarcastic smile on her face, and said, "You have connection up in heaven right? So ask Him to heal me". I surprised myself with what I just said to her, I was sure that the Holy Spirit just spoke through me. I told her, "By the time you arrive at your dentist, the swelling on your cheek and your teeth will be healed."

It was almost 4:30 pm and I was getting ready to leave work when the phone rang and my supervisor told me that it was for me. I answered the phone and it was Cori on the other end. With a screaming voice she said, "Shadhona by the time I came to my dentist my swelling completely went away and my teeth are completely healed. Wow! You do have connection up in Heaven." I just realized I had the gift of prophecy and I thanked God for using me to heal her. Next Sunday, when I arrived at church, I saw Cori and her sister sitting in the church and they yelled out my name. With a smile on her face, I could see that she was so happy to see me. With a big smile she said, "Look, I am actually in your church." It was truly a miracle to see this.

It was like God was answering my prayers like popcorn popping. Let me explain: the pot is my heart, the oil is the anointing of the Holy Spirit; the corn is my prayer and without the heat that corn will never pop; the heat is my faith in Christ. A few days later, God gave me a dream. In my dream, I saw that my youngest brother who also came to Canada with us too, died, and the hospital called me and gave me the news. I saw the hallway of the hospital that I was walking in was a kidney-shaped hallway. The nurse was leading me to his body. In my dream I asked them where his clothes were and they showed me that they were under the bed where his body was laying. I looked and saw white clothing with red blood on it. Three days after I had the dream, I was woken up by a phone call at 3 in the morning. I was half-asleep and picked up the phone on the other end it was the hospital calling me to tell me that my brother had an accident and to please come over. I repeatedly asked, "How bad is it?"

The nurse replied, "It is really bad but I would rather tell you in person." I insisted she tell me over the phone.

She said, "He passed away." I was still learning English, thought she meant he fainted—passed out. When I arrived at the hospital, the nurse took me down through a kidney shaped hallway I instantly recalled my dream. As I came to the room where he was, I saw him. He passed away means he was dead, I asked where his clothing was, they pointed me under his bed, I grabbed them only they were not white; they were black, and then I saw a Bible. I immediately looked inside to see who gave it to him because that was important to me. I saw the people who gave him the Bible were evangelical Christians. I pondered on the dream God gave me and what it meant. The meaning came to me later on, the white clothing with blood on it that I saw in my dream was "the blood of Jesus that cleansed his sins as white as the white sheet I saw, and the Bible was the confirmation that my brother knew Jesus before he left this earth.

Shadhona

CHAPTER 10

Evangelist David Wilkerson's conference in Copps Collisium

In 1982 spring, our church announced that, Evangelist David Wilkerson is coming to Copps Collisium and he also is an author of the book "Cross and the switch blade." I decided to go with few friends, though it would be a nice evening out with friends. There were thousands of people attending
this night. I was overwhelmed how packed out the collisium was. After a lot of announcement and singing I saw Mr. Wilkerson take the podium, soon after he started speaking, I was so impressed with him, he was bold and right to the point and his message was very convicting to my spirit. I was totally captivated by every word he was saying. I was practically eating his words. I was thinking to myself." I wish I could meet him in person, then I thought in this house of thousands of people it is impossible."

Then my faith said "If Jesus wants me to meet him He will even bring him my way and I will meet him."

After Mr. Wilkerson finished his message at the end he gave an open invitation to anyone who was interested in joining him in an outreach in Southern California in summer for two weeks, to fill out an application form before they leave. I right away decided to sign up for it ,and prayed that ,if Jesus wants me to go my application will be chosen. Just in Edmonton, three hundred people applied David Wilkerson selected only two from Edmonton; I was one of the two. Mr. Wilkerson promised that .our lives would never be the same again and we will be sharing our experiences for years to come. I decided to save up money from here on for my summer trip, and took an extra week for my vacation from work. I arrived in Los Angeles in July, and I was picked up by one of the staff from Teen Challenge ministry. I stayed at the University of Southern California at the dorm.

Shadhona

Chapter 11

Outreach in L.A California

𝒯his morning, my first day in this outreach, we all got in a van and headed to a church near downtown, going out to share the gospel of Jesus. I was very nervous as we all walked inside the church. Shortly after, the pastor of this church announced the speaker for that morning, his name was Larry Pate. As we listened to him speak I was really happy and pleased for the kind of message he gave us, it made me feel better and less nervous. After the meeting, everybody went outside to get their specific area, and some were talking to the speaker. I was very talkative getting here, and usually I love to talk, but this morning after the meeting, something supernatural happened to me, I tried to open my mouth, but were not able to. My tongue felt stuck, and the Holy Spirit told me to move toward where the speaker was who was talking to others. I made my way to him, but still could not speak. Mr. Pate looked at me and came toward me saying "Hi, what's your name? By now I was crying and still had a hard time talking. Then the most astonishing thing happened he started speaking in my language, and all of a sudden my tongue was released and I was able to speak. The Lord knew if I was able to move my tongue I would have followed the girls I just met and gone outside and talked to them. God wanted me to meet Larry for a reason. From talking to him I found out he lived in my hometown Dhaka Bangladesh for ten years and knows my language fluently. He then invited me to come to his house and met his wife after I completed my two weeks. Soon we became very good friends. One day while we were out in Venice area, Larry Pate came to me and said, "I want you to meet someone."

I said, "Who?" he smiled and took me right to Mr. David Wilkerson. I was breathless, and instantly had a flashback of when David Wilkerson came to Edmonton and while listening to his magnificent message I was wishing to meet him in person and shake his hand, then realized how impossible it would be with tens of thousands of people in this coliseum and told my friends with me, "If God wants me to meet him He will bring him to me." Here I am in front of him shaking his hands and then I said to him, "Wait you are not going anywhere unless you sign my Bible." He smiled then signed my Bible.

Shadhona

Chapter 12

My memorable day Witnessing

This morning after the seminar, our leader put us in groups of two and sent us to this subdivision where mostly Jewish people lived. I was sent here also with my male partner Keith. We took different streets and planned to meet at a certain spot. It was a rich neighborhood, big mansions with big iron bar gates, and very high gates. I have never seen big mansions like these before. So I started knocking doors as I passed by each house, even though this made me very uncomfortable. I don't like bothering people in their private homes, but I am here to do what is required of me by the organization. Most people after I knocked would not even open their gate. They would look through the peeping hole on the gate, all I could see was one eye through that peeping hole and they would say "What do you want?" I had to share the gospel of Jesus through that hole and most of them were not interested in what I had to say, but they took the flyer I handed out. It was a flyer about the movie "Cross and the Switch Blade" that we showed every night for these two weeks. At the end of my morning, it was the last house on the end of the street, I knocked, I was hungry and was parched, it is 90 degrees here in L.A. To my amazement someone actually opened the door, it was an elderly lady. Before I could say a word, she said, "Today the messiah is here, I have been praying for the messiah to come to me since my husband passed away two years ago." I was dumbfounded. Wow! She actually saw Jesus through me. She invited me in, another surprise because all the other houses didn't even let me in.

    I came in and sat down. She offered me something to drink and I asked for water I was beyond thirsty. She brought me a glass of cold water, holding it with her frail hand that was shaking as she handed it to me. I gulped it down very fast, she smiled at me. I then took a breath and then shared with her why I was there to share with her about Jesus, the Messiah she just confirmed that she was praying for. I witnessed to her and asked her if she would receive Jesus as her Lord and Savior she replied, "Yes of course I have been waiting for this day. I felt like a million bucks, when I left her house, it was all worth it walking in this heat all morning when no one even responded to me, but this one lady her accepting Christ made it all a successful day.

    On my way back to the tent where we all met around noon to go back to the dorm, I had to stop at a red light; it was a big intersection. As I was waiting for the green light to cross over, I looked to my left and saw a man sitting on a bench by a bus stop. I was so hungry all I could think was to go to my dorm and go for lunch. I heard the voice in my head Jesus speaking to me saying, "Go and ask him to accept me as his Lord and Savior." I was so shocked at what I just heard I wanted to make sure it was the Lord speaking to me, so I said back, "Lord, you want me just to go and ask him to accept you just like that? You mean no conversation the four spiritual laws or have few words to feel him out and then maybe ask? The Lord spoke to me again and said, "Yes just like that ask him to receive me as his Lord and Savior; he has been waiting all his life." I thought it is very important to me to obey God, even if this is making me very uncomfortable and I might be making a fool of myself to this stranger. If this isn't God speaking to me, but I rather make a fool of myself and obey God than miss out on His call and disobey Him. So slowly, I walked up to him and said, "Sir, what I am about to tell you might seem crazy to you, but, I have to do this I have to ask you, "Would like to accept Jesus as your Lord and Savior?"

He immediately responded by saying, "Yes I would." Just at time his bus arrived, and I was relieved and said to him, "Your bus is here maybe you can think about this when you go home." What he told me next gave me shivers and the confirmation that it was really Jesus speaking to me.

This man said to me, "No let the bus go I have been waiting my whole life for this," exactly what the Lord told me. I handed him a card that had the name of an evangelical church near where he lives and requested that he hand this to the pastor of this church when he decides to go. This is something David Wilkerson did make these cards of every evangelical church in Southern California, so after someone accepts Christ we handed them one of these cards. I was literally skipping my way into the tent where we report anything special for that morning to our leaders before we head back to the dorm. Wow! What a glorious morning I had, thank you Jesus I love you. I went to the tent and reported about the sweet Jewish lady and the man at the bus stop, I will remember this as long as I live. After I shared my incredible morning with them and the leaders we hopped in the van and came back to the dorm .Our schedule is same every day for this two weeks. Seminar in the morning then go to the subdivisions, after lunch we worked around downtown, and Santa Monica Blvd, and after supper from eight o'clock till sometimes one or two in the morning in Hollywood Blvd and Beverly Hills. The only time I have few hours of free time is after lunch for an hour before we go to the downtown area.

Shadhona

Chapter 13

Miracle

This morning during my early morning devotion, I asked Jesus for something very specific. I prayed that when I go out there to share the gospel, before even I speak a word, the people will actually see His LOVE. After lunch, James and I were designated to downtown L.A. He is my partner for the afternoon. After the van dropped us off we headed toward the busy side of the town, but every time James saw an antique store he went inside just to browse. After he went to quite a few stores, I asked him "James would you do this to your boss at work, in the middle of working would you step out to go antique shopping?" He replied, "Absolutely not."

Then I said, "Why are you treating God this way?" We are here working for God and you are taking so many breaks. He apologized, then we decided to go our separate way and once we were done, we were going to meet at a certain spot. I went my way, talked

Miracle

to many people about God's love through Jesus and many accepted Christ as I prayed the salvation prayer with them. Finally when I was done, and it was time to head back, I started to go toward where I am supposed to meet James. As I was turning to that corner, I could hear a loud female voice swearing everything under the sun, at someone, once I turned the corner I noticed, she is swearing at James. Next what happened was a true miracle. As I was approaching them, this elderly lady looked at me and immediately started weeping, and once I got near to where she was, she fell down on her knees before me and broke down in tears and was still crying, I quickly picked her up to her feet and pleaded with her not to do this. I am just like her. Then she shared with me, that she is about to lose her puppies she kept at this catholic church for all this time, now that she can't pay rent anymore they are going to get rid of her puppies. So I gave her enough money to save her puppies till she finds a more permanent place. I know normally we are not supposed to give money to strangers, but this time, I felt the leading of the Holy Spirit. Then I asked her if she knows Jesus as her Savior, she said that she didn't I then asked her if she would like to accept Him as her Lord and Savior, she said that she would, and prayed the prayer of salvation with her.

This entire time, I noticed, James stood there, still, and very quiet. I thought maybe the reason he was not saying anything is because of what just happened. The lady was swearing at him, but, when I came along, she was so receptive. It was a very long awkward walk. When we arrived at the tent, we were given refreshments before heading to the dorm. The leaders asked if anyone had any praise reports. To my surprise, James got up and as he started to share, I was having goose bumps. He said, "Today I went with Shadhona to the downtown area and we decided to go our separate ways for a while. When we were done I was waiting for her to meet me at the spot we arranged to meet after we were done. While I was waiting for her, an elderly lady came over and I was trying to talk to her, but she seemed angry and was swearing at me, with everything under the sun. Then we saw Shadhona walking toward us, and I saw a BIG WAVE of God's LOVE just coming toward us and the closer she got the more the powerful the wave felt. The elderly lady started to weep the moment she saw Shadhona, and as she got closer to us, the lady fell down on her knees before Shadhona, and completely broke down in tears, and Shadhona picked her up and within minutes started talking to her, and gave her the invitation to accept Christ and the lady accepted Jesus as her Lord and Savior. I wasn't able to open my mouth until now. I jumped out of my chair and shouted out to all, what I asked Jesus this morning during my devotion, I told them I asked Jesus that today I wanted people to see His love before I even speak a word. Everybody was so excited and we all felt the presence of the Holy Spirit and gave God all the praise and glory for what He has done.

Shadhona

Chapter 14

Hollywood night

Today is my last Friday at the Hollywood at nighttime. Today I was assigned with Keith who is my partner for the day and night. This afternoon we went to Beverly hills Wiltshire Blvd. As I was walking down Beverly hills and was admiring these multi-million dollar homes I was just crossing a driveway by the side walk and a huge gate on my left opened up, and black limousine was slowly coming out of this big mansion, as I was star struck, looking I forgot to move, so the driver rolled the window down and asked me to move, I looked in and saw a man sitting in the back seat. I directly looked at him and said, "Sir may I speak to you?"

He answered, "What do you want my dear?"

I said, "I just want to talk to you sir for few minutes?" To my surprise he actually stepped out of his big fancy limousine and stood in front of me. I was looking at a man who is 6ft. 8 inches. My neck was hurting trying to look at him, so I respectfully asked, "Sir can you go down on your knees I can barely look at your eyes my neck is killing me." So he did.

Then he said to me, "Be quick to whatever you have to say. I am going to a billion dollar meeting." I had no idea how much billion dollar is.

I quickly said to him, "Sir you can have all the money in the world, but what good would it so to you when you leave this earth? Wouldn't it be much better and meaningful to your life if you have Jesus as your Lord and Savior, then He will give you the peace and joy for you to enjoy your wealth and have it all. This way you go to Heaven when you die, you don't lose anything. He can even bless you for this meeting you are going to, and give you wisdom as to how to invest your wealth." He thought for a while and while on his knees he asked me how he can receive this Jesus I am talking about. I was so excited, I smiled and prayed with him the salvation prayer, and he accepted Jesus as his Lord and Savior, when he was leaving he smiled at me and I said to him, "Remember with Jesus in your life you can never lose."

Tonight supper tasted really good, or maybe I was so starved, that anything would taste good. I had few minutes to rest before heading to Hollywood tonight. I went to my room and actually fell asleep. My roommate woke me up; I had to get ready really fast, and jump in the van and Keith is my partner tonight. Keith and I went right near Wiltshire Blvd and what I witnessed next was like watching a horror movie. I saw men and women were being thrown out like flying saucers, this biker gang, almost 25 of them were there and were throwing these people out of the restaurant because they wanted to be in there. They were all wearing leather jackets with a logo on them "Hell's Angels".

Keith told me, "Let's go. The van will pick us up. It's right around the corner from this street."

I said "No. God wants me to go and tell their leader that Jesus loves him."

Keith replied, "Just before we got here a woman was witnessing to them and one of the guys pulled her hair and threw her across the street, now let's go."

I said to him, "Sorry you go ahead I have to obey God, I have to go and tell their leader that Jesus loves him."

Keith finally ran away, without me. I walked up and said to them, "Excuse me who is your leader?" One of the women pointed me to this tall guy he looked like a Goliath, I walked up to him, and because he was so tall, I had to pull on his jacket to get his attention.

He bent down a bit and said to me, "What do you want?"

I said to him, "I just wanted you to know that, JESUS LOVS YOU."

He looked in the sky and throwing his hands up he shouted, "Why me?" After sharing that I, walked away and then started running toward where the van is supposed to be, and they were all waiting for me.

Keith immediately asked me, with a sarcastic voice, "So were you able to tell him what God told you to?"

I said, "You better believe it" and Keith was so surprised that I was still in one piece and no harm was done to me.

Shadhona

CHAPTER 15

Last day in L.A.

Today, I was giddy all day, I think it's because I hardly had any sleep after I came back from Hollywood. I was also excited that it this two-week journey was finally over and I get to go home next Monday. This morning after the seminar, the leaders were going to send us to this very dangerous black neighbourhood. One of the leaders called on all the black women, and asked them to take off all their jewellery, and asked all the black men to partner up with these women. As they were leaving he looked at me and said, "Shadhona go with them." I jumped out of my seat and ran and joined them. When we arrived at this neighbourhood I noticed that there was a picture of a big skeleton on an entrance to the street of this neighbourhood and there was inscription that read, NO WHITE MAN WALKED IN HERE AND CAME OUT ALIVE. I never thought that, my skin being chocolate milk can be a positive thing and be helpful.

Last day in L.A.

I went in with my partner Keith, and as he was talking to someone, I walked around and came across this man who was under the hood of his car, working in his car. I greeted with a hello and he jumped right out from under his car and pointed a gun at me. I gently told him, "You don't have to point that at me, I just wanted to invite you to a movie David Wilkerson is showing tonight called "The Cross and the Switch Blade" here at the school gym in your neighbourhood." He still had the gun pointed and, after I requested to move it away from my face, he did.

He said, "Sure", so I shared with him about the love of Jesus and how He died for his sin, and had risen on the third day, and if he accepts Jesus as his Lord and Savior, he can live with Jesus in eternity in Heaven. After talking to him for a while he finally put the gun away.

Then I said again to him, "You see your gun is a sign of weakness to me, because you need an external force to communicate with me, and not with the power of your mind. Also if you shoot me and it is not my time to go yet, I will not die and you would have lost a bullet and also go to jail, I will still be alive and free. Then again, if you shoot me and it is my time to go, I will die but go to Heaven to live with Jesus in eternity, and you still will be in jail. See it's a win-win for me." He got angry but I could see the frustration in him that he knew what I was saying was nothing but the TRUTH. I handed him the flyer and told him that I hoped to see him tonight. After we were done for the day, we went back to the dorm after supper hopped in the van as usual and headed to this black neighbourhood to show the film. David Wilkerson and all the leaders were at the front of this big gym, 7 pm, nobody was coming— just the leaders. And now I am looking at the big clock 7:30pm, still silence, no one is coming. All of a sudden, I saw this guy I was talking to this afternoon, who pointed his gun at me, walk through the door, and with him was his entire gang, and many other gang members showed up. So finally we showed the film and many of these men gave their life to Jesus, what a night. I was pumped to see such a victorious night.

Shadhona

Chapter 16

Last day in Hollywood

Today is Saturday, the last day for this outreach. Today I went to downtown, and Venice, at the beach, they call it a "muscle beach". I witnessed to many people about Jesus and so many people men and women, came to know Jesus as their Savior. We went back to the dorm and after a short rest had supper and for the last time went to Hollywood, and tonight the street was packed with hundreds of people, it is the week end night, a party night here. As I was walking by with my partner, I thought I saw something move inside this big garbage, as I looked again, I saw a young woman stand up from inside the garbage bin. I said hello to her and asked what her name was she replied "Mary Magdelene."

"Happy birthday, here is a dollar maybe you can buy yourself ice cream." I replied.

To my surprise she replied "No thank you, I don't want your money, but you can sing me a birthday song."

I couldn't believe she wanted me to sing in Hollywood street in the middle of this crowed people, so I looked around there many people heard us and decided to stop and see what I was going to do. I cleared my singing voice and sang the birthday song for her. Good the work is done. I still offered her my dollar to go and treat herself with some ice cream.

She responded again and what she wanted shocked me, she said, "I don't want your money. I want a hug from you." I am thinking to myself no way, there was stuff hanging from her head and she is sitting in a garbage bin. I am going to die with the smell, so I quickly asked Jesus to close my sense of smell when I hug her "please Lord". So I asked her to come out and what happened next few minutes was God intervention. The moment I reached my arms out and the moment I hugged her, I didn't smell any bad odour, what I felt for the first time. I felt the COMPASSION of God. After, I hugged her I offered her the women's shelter and she gladly accepted.

It's after midnight, I was walking toward the area where the van was parked, to pick us up, on my way there I was thinking, all my imaginations about Hollywood being so glamorous, and a paradise completely wiped out, once I saw the real Hollywood I nothing like that, after what my eyes have seen these past two weeks, it is hell on earth. I got in the van, and once everybody came in we headed back to the dorm, usually I am always very talkative, but, tonight I couldn't shake off what I saw and feeling the compassion of God as I hugged this homeless woman. Once I arrived at the dorm I wanted to make sure I was somewhat ready when I leave, so I did my laundry till four in the morning, thinking that I will sleep in tomorrow. On this last Sunday, David Wilkerson gave us this day off and also paid for as many of us that wanted to go to Disney World this day. I decided to stay back and have the day to myself. I recently found out that behind this university there was a huge rose garden, and this is where they take roses from during the Rose Bowl. So I thought of walking down these rose bushes and having a peaceful day, just Jesus and I.

Brenda my roommate asked me if she could hang out with me she said, "I just want to spend the day with you would that be okay?" I didn't want her with me, I already made my awesome plan, but, I decided to be kind and included her in my day, but didn't go to the rose garden. So after everybody left this morning to the Disney World, I told Brenda that because the cafeteria is closed; we have to go out for breakfast. As we were walking down the sidewalk, I noticed a young man sitting under a tree strangely enough in sack cloth, and in a short distance a police officer sitting in his car. As I was walking by this man under the tree, he started running after me saying some strange words in some strange language, sounded like gibberish to me, and Brenda got scared and started running for the dorm.

I turned around and stopped and said out loud "Brenda I rebuke you in the name of Jesus get back here," and she did, then I looked at this man who was now right in front of me still speaking weird words to me, I looked at him and said, "In the name of JESUS I rebuke you" and immediately this man fell down at my feet. By now the officer who was in his car watching this, ran toward me with one hand holding his holster where his gun is.

He came up to me and asked me, "How did you do this?"

I replied to him saying, "In the name of Jesus I did this. The Bible says that every knee shall bow and every tongue shall confess that Jesus is the CHRIST." The officer smiled, and then I told him that I didn't want have any charge against this man, but he probably needs something to eat and drink some water, if he wouldn't mind getting it to him, cause by the time I come back from having my breakfast, I would be a long time. The police officer agreed to take care of him. When I was walking back to the dorm I noticed the same young man sitting under that tree looking very peaceful, and he even smiled at me as I walked by him. I am so glad I didn't go to the Disney World, I would have missed this God moment.

Shadhona

CHAPTER 17

Riverside California

Soon after I came home from Los Angeles, I started saving money. First thing I did, prayed about my attending Bible school, I know this would require me to give up my job, and also my beautiful big apartment. It was very clear to me that God would want me to accept their offer to attend Teen Challenge Ministry Institute. In December 1982 I quit my job at the Worker's Compensation Board, and also gave my land lady notice of my leave from this apartment at the end of December. I moved to a much smaller, a studio apartment and at the same time added my younger sister to stay there sometimes, and also mom came back from Bangladesh and wanted to stay with me for a while.

She always went to Bangladesh in winter and lived in Edmonton during summer time. Mom was having problem with her legs, she went from walking with a cane to wheelchair. During this time I asked Jesus to use me to heal her legs. I asked mom if she would let me massage her legs every day, for a month, and see if she gets healed; she gladly took my offer. As I started massaging her legs two weeks in to it, she came out her wheel chair and started walking with a walker I was amazed because, I knew that each time I massaged I prayed that, God would heal her legs. After two weeks of my massages, my mom left the walker and started using a cane. I was so excited I shared with her that. I was praying that. Jesus would heal her. She smiled at me and I was relieved she didn't take offense to that. Few days later my mom told me that she wanted to show me something. I went to the hallway and near the staircase. She dropped the cane and walked down and up the staircase without the cane, I shouted praise the LORD, I couldn't help it.

During dialysis mom was having problem go to the washroom naturally, they had to use a catheter to help her pass urine. I asked if she would mind if pastor Johnson came and prayed for her, to my surprise, she agreed. Since pastor Mcknight left the church to be the head executive for the Penticostal Assembly of Canada in Toronto, pastor Johnson filled the position as our new pastor. I asked if Pastor Johnson would come to the hospital and pray for mom, he said yes that he would. When he arrived and stood at my mom's bedside, I explained to mom that he was going to pray in the name of Jesus, and as he held mom's tiny hand he stared praying and I was holding her other hand. All of a sudden she was healed and the nurses wanted us to move and put the curtain all around mom. She is healed! Since then she was able to go to the washroom naturally! I gave the apartment to my younger sister and left her enough money for rent till I got back and also to take care of mom till she goes to Bangladesh. I left for Riverside in a cold morning at the end of January, was really glad to leave this cold and go to sunny California.

Shadhona

CHAPTER 18

Dreams, visions and miracles in this Castle

I realized very quickly that I loved theology class and history classes the best. At my theology class, my teacher gave an assignment after two months into his teaching. He wanted us to write an essay that is our testimony and to be creative in writing it, also to use as many metaphors and to use allegory. He also said that, he would read the top three in the class. I prayed that night, before I went to bed and asked Jesus that I would like mine to be one of the three that he reads. I told Jesus, all my life in elementary and high school I wasn't a very good student I only got A on religion subject and history. I had two weeks for this project to complete. Few days later I had a DREAM. In my dream, I saw my theology teacher received all our essay and announced the top three essays, and my essay was one of the top three. When I woke up, I knew Jesus gave me the dream to assure me that He heard me and I have the answer to my prayers, even though I doubted at first for few second. Two weeks later, we handed in our essays and next day the teacher brought in our essays, I know this is a BIG day for me, I also shared my dream with my study group, they all looked at me when the teacher announced the top three, and mine was one of the three, I screamed saying, "YES" the teacher looked at me, so I shared with him and the whole class my prayer and how Jesus answered my prayer through a dream. I couldn't believe my ears as I heard him read my essay as one of the top three. It is Tuesday it's Chapel day today. Six in the morning I was in that dry wall and musty smelly room having my devotion.

All of a sudden in this almost dark room, I saw a VISION from the Lord. Like a screen an area of the room lit up, its bright light, and I saw a red rose flower and it fell to the ground and with it also fell a veil over it, and the room was filled with the fragrance of the rose. I was so taken by this vision and the smell of this rose that, I was at awe and I am mesmerised. During breakfast I shared my vision with few of my girlfriends. When I came to the chapel, as I was sitting down one of my class mate "Luis" as he was passing by looked me and shouted out saying, "Hey Shadhona do you know that, you are a FRAGRANCE of Chris Jesus?" I was so excited at his comment I could barely contain myself. My friends who knew about my vision were also sharing the joy with me. When the Chapel service started one of our teacher Pat came and read the scripture for the day, and as he read the scripture verse I had shivers all over me. This is for sure my second and final confirmation after what Luis said to me earlier, my teacher Pat read 2nd Corinthian Chapter 2:15, it says, "For we are a fragrance of Christ to God among those who are being saved and among those who are perishing." So awesome I have the confirmation of the vision Jesus gave me.

It's Easter weekend, and I realized that I brought only few nice attire with me and I was really wishing that I had a nice out fit to wear for Easter Sunday. Having very few clothing, i prayed and asked Jesus if He would provide for me a turquoise blouse and a white skirt for me. I also realize it would have to be a miracle, there is no mall nearby, and i have no transportation to even get to one and the most importantly I didn't bring enough money to buy myself a nice outfit. It's Saturday morning, and I was doing my usual chores in the morning, today I got the job of vacuuming and dusting. The phone was ringing and I couldn't hear it because, I was vacuuming. One of my roommates came and told me that the call is for me. I stopped and went to the living room to answer the phone, on the other end I hear Mary Pate's voice I was so happy to hear her voice, I said, "Hello? Hi how are you? So glad to hear your voice."

She replied, "Well today I am taking you shopping."

I thought how does she know I want to buy an outfit? So I asked her, "How did you know that I need a new outfit?

She replied, "The Lord told me that you need to go shopping, because you need clothes, so here I am." I was so shocked, so I shared with her about my prayers—a special wish for Easter. Mary took me to the mall and told me that the Lord wants her to pay for anything I want to buy, so to start shopping. Wow! I was like a kid running around the mall to find exactly what I wished for. I found my turquoise blouse and my white skirt and when I went to the cashier, Mary handed in her credit card and paid for it and when I thanked her she smiled and said to me "don't thank me, thank Jesus He is the one who sent me to take you shopping and to buy you anything you wanted." When she brought me back to the dorm, I couldn't stop smiling, I felt so special this is truly a MIRACLE. Sunday morning I got up still at awe at what happened yesterday, and I wore my new blouse and skirt to the Easter service feeling all SPECIAL.

This week I graduate, it's June and this is my last month in this beautiful castle. I graduated with B plus and I am more than happy to get an A plus on my essay and to have it read by my teacher as one of the top three is enough to make me more than happy. On the graduation day me and my study group took lots of pictures and it was a beautiful day, as we were just hanging out outside by the garden, few of the girls already left with their parents who attended the graduation ceremony. Few of us were still left here because we have to catch a plane soon. As I was taking pictures and talking to my few friends and saying our goodbyes, all of sudden I heard a loud scream, we all rushed back by the big valley. The workers were doing some cleaning around the bush and the valley and they found a big snake that came out of this big rock and with its babies. Wait did they say snake? I am afraid of snakes. Ever since I was a child back in Bangladesh one afternoon as we were having our afternoon tea, a snake charmer was in front of the veranda doing his tricks and as he was playing the flute the cobra snake came out of the basket and instead of dancing to his music, decided to take off right through the veranda into our living room. Half of him was still outside when the snake charmer pulled him away, I still remember I jumped up and grabbed the iron bar above my head and hung there till the snake was out and in his basket. I can't sleep even if I watch a cartoon movie if there is a snake in it. I stayed farther than everyone else to see this excitement, as my classmates were taking pictures. When I looked at the rock where the snake came from under, I had the shock of my life. This is the very rock I sat on many days to have my quite time and my devotion during my spare time, and all this time this was the snake's nest. Not once did it go under it, or come out of the rock while I was sitting on this rock, Jesus protected me all this time. I took the evening flight to come home to Edmonton.

Shadhona

Chapter 19

Coming to Ridge way Ontario

Shortly after I came back to Edmonton, I was taking time to make a decision for my life. I was thinking do I go back to my normal life by getting my old job back, or do I serve God by putting to practice with the training and diploma I earned for these past few months. I felt a real sense of peace when I made the decision to serve God with my training. I was searching for a Christian women's institution where I could work with these women in need of counselling. Through much searching, I found out that the only women's Rehab Centre was in Ontario. I was willing to go anyplace. So I applied for the job, at this rehab Centre in Ridgeway Ontario.

Prior to my sending an application, I never heard of Ridgeway before. So I asked people in my Church if they knew anything about this place. Most people told me that Ridgeway is near Niagara Falls. I asked what is the Falls, and it had to be explained to me. So I told my mom who didn't want me to leave, she desperately tried to change my mind, but I felt very sure about my decision. I shared my plan with my youth group and my youth pastor Billy Richard. The week end before my leave, I was walking down the river with this young man John. It was a very nice Saturday for September. As I stood near the water, I saw a vision and in this vision, I saw myself speaking to a big crowd of people, and there was a big globe behind and above me. Each time the globe turned, the crowd changed to a different crowd of people. I was so fascinated by the vision and I was sure that it was from God. Not totally understanding the vision, I told John, "Hey John, I just had a vision, I think it means that I will travel all around the world and share my testimony." John was very excited for me as I was mentoring him by his request, before I left for Ontario. On Sunday after church, Pastor Billy pulled me aside and asked me to come see him next week.

I am embarrassed to admit that when he asked to come and see him, I assumed maybe the youth group collected a donation for me because they know I quit my job and was short for cash.

When I arrived at his office, he asked me to sit down and then, handed me an envelope full of money, and said to me, "The youth collected this money for you and asked me to give it to you." Then he handed me a form and asked me to sign it, so he can mail it before I leave for Ontario. I was puzzled, and asked, "What is this I am signing?"

He replied, "Have you heard of Hundred Huntley Street?"

I said, "No."

He then said, "I used to be a camera man for this Christian television Ministry, I told them they have to hear your testimony, so you have to sign this form so they know that you are going to accept their invitation to appear on their show."

I was very excited that, he wanted me to share my story on television. On November 18 1983, I came to Ontario and arrived at the Ridgeway Rehab Centre very late at night. When I applied for this job, there was one condition and that was that they wouldn't offer me a full time commitment for the job. I had three months' probation before a full time position was offered to me. I was fine with it. Three months after this probation period, I realized home mission is not for me. Evangelism is to go out in the world and share my testimony, that is my gift and calling. The very next day after I arrived, I received a phone call from 100 Huntley Street Ministry. They invited me to come and be their guest on their television show and David Mainse was going to interview me. I gladly accepted. On December 5th, I went to Toronto and appeared on the 100 Huntley Street television show. The next day I received hundreds of mails from all around the world. This show was on air in different countries in different days. All of a sudden it came clear to me the vision Jesus gave me when I was walking by the river in Edmonton. How amazing is my Savior's love for me.

Three months into my working here I decided that I would not commit to work here for a year, so I let the director know my decision to leave after my three months was over. I had no plan or idea as to where I would go from there. The ninety-acre property in this facility was magnificent, just tall trees and trees as far as your eyes can see. I was thinking where the fruit trees were. While in Edmonton, I had a dream that, I was in a farm and on a ladder picking fruits and there were vineyards all around me. After I left Ridgeway, I went to Vineland where Ed and his lovely wife live. I shared with them that I need a place to stay. Ed and his wife are well known in this Niagara region, especially in Vineland. Ed was highly esteemed, I wasn't aware of that, and because I was associated with Ed, many people opened their homes to me till, I could find a more permanent place. I finally found a room and board place in a home near a few churches. Since I only knew Ed, I attended his church. Since my appearance on Hundred Huntley Street, I was invited by pastor Henry Wiebe, in his church "the Mountain View Church". This the first time I met Pastor Wiebe, a very charismatic preacher. After I shared my testimony at his church, many doors of opportunity were opened for me to share my testimony in many churches from different denominations all across the Niagara region. Very quickly I came to find out that, Pastor Henry Wiebe was highly respected and revered by Mennonite churches all across Canada and especially here in Niagara region. I left Ridgeway in February and in the spring I found a job on a grape farm tying grapevines. I did this job till the end of July. Farm jobs aren't for me. Now it was very clear to me that, God gave me this dream in Edmonton just before I left, the dream where I was working in a fruit farm. I had no knowledge prior to coming to Ridgeway that, Niagara region is known for their vineyards. Pastor Henry Wiebe is still today my mentor and my spiritual counsellor, I am so blessed. God always goes a head of me and prepares people to care for me.

Shadhona

Chapter 20

Moving to a nearby city

$\mathcal{L}$iving in a small town like Vineland became very difficult for me to have a good job. After my eight-month-contract expired I decided to move to a nearby city. Having a car which Ed and Thelma helped me purchase, came handy. Shortly after I moved to this city I was told that, the city I came to is considered a VALLEY. I thought to myself really? Wow, this the vision Jesus gave me when I was sitting in my home church in Edmonton. The vision, where I was stuck in a big valley and I had a pair of shorts and a blouse, this indicated the season, that, it would be summer. I was running back and forth, because I heard a loud trumpet sound and all the people were running toward the sound of the trumpet and they were shouting and saying that, "Jesus is here!" As I was running back and forth, I was crying out to Jesus and in this vision I saw a big long hand that shined like a bright white light. The hand came down right where I was and I heard a voice in my head saying

"I always heard you when you cried out to me." Even today when I mention this vision, my eyes gets all teary. I rented a room and board, and found a part time job for a few months and kept working in different places as part time work and I was getting very frustrated at not finding a permanent job. Here in Ontario contract jobs are more available than a full time job.

In 1987 I decided to volunteer in an elementary school while looking for job again. I was desperate and looking for a place to rent again. The other people I lived with were moving and had to leave. It was the last day of February and I had to move out on this on this last day. On Wednesday, I walked in a church and I saw a room full of women and there was food and coffee. After grabbing some food and coffee, being so hungry, I sat down. After shoving the food down, I asked a lady, "who is the leader here?" She pointed her to me, I went up to her and asked her if she could announce to this group of women , if anyone has a room for rent. She was very gracious and handed me the microphone and I got up and shared with these women that, I was desperate for a room for rent, and preferably an elderly lady, where I could do her chores in exchange of rent. I walked away disappointed no one had a room for me, but I still trusted that, God would take care of me. I reflected on the dream He gave me in Edmonton, where I was walking up the staircase of a hospital and noticed a ring with a green cross on it on my engagement finger. I know that Jesus is going to take care of me. I felt very anxious time is running out in me, I have to find a place today. As I turned the corner of this small hallway to walk out, I crossed a young woman, tall and blonde.

She passed me and then stopped and said to me, "Did anybody give you a place to stay?"

I replied, "No"

She then said, "With all these women in the room no one gave you a place to stay?"

I said, "No, I would sleep in my car if it wasn't February. Too cold."

She then stopped again and said, "No don't sleep in your car. Listen, me and my family are going away to Florida for ten days you can come and stay at my house."

As she was walking away I yelled, "Wait what's your name and where do you live?"

She smiled and yelled out as she was walking way "Arsenau is my last name I am in the phone book and I live in Chetland Crescent. The rest was history. Cathy let me stay at her house for six months free of rent. She refused to take any money from me, knowing that I was living on very small amount of unemployment insurance.

The first day she showed me her kitchen and said, "I don't like to cook so don't expect me to cook for you, if you want anything here is my fridge and here is everything in the kitchen, feel free to eat, but you can help yourself."

I laughed so hard; she was so honest. I told her, "I love to cook. Is it okay if I cook for you and your family?" She gave me a big smile and said "any time". Soon after, I cooked for the family and did babysitting whenever she needed. I was almost a second mom to her three cute kids, Nicole, Michelle and her only baby boy Nathan. Soon after, we went from good friends to best friends. The Arsenaus became like a family for the first time since I left Edmonton. In my opinion, Cathy's middle name should be "COMPASSION." Very seldom have I met anyone so compassionate like Cathy.

Shadhona

CHAPTER 21

Living in the Valley

Many months have gone by and my health seems to be getting no better. The injury I got from the car accident in my back, neck, and my knees, now I am having chronic pain from my bone joints, also I am not able to read for long as it really hurts my neck. Also, I can only sit for a short time and stand for a short time. I began to notice how slowly my movement was very limited, and also my life had come almost to a halt with the limitation I now had. Months have gone by and I'm still able to do very little as far as any movement, or doing any meaningful job. I did housekeeping for a short while until I hurt my back again. This time I decided to take no risks with my health, so I decided to do the bare minimum, even as I did volunteer jobs. Now a few years have gone by, still I am not able to have a job, but, thank God, He took care of me as He promised, At least I have my disability temporarily. As the years went on, I began to feel stuck in this valley of life, both physically and spiritually. I was starting to feel so down emotionally, and feeling stuck in this valley of life both physically and spiritually. I was asked by my church, if I would be willing to sing a song in the early service, which was more casual. We called it a "Community Service". I accepted as I was always willing to serve when opportunity came my way. I decided to write a song from my heart about what I was going through at this time, and I used a Bangladeshi folk melody to it and played my (tabla) as I sang the song. This was truly the cry of my heart. Here are the lyrics to my heartfelt cry to Jesus.

> Jesus I am crying out to you from this deep valley.
> I have been trapped in this valley for so many years and one by one they all have left me, when I cried for their help. Jesus I am crying out to you from this deep valley.
> My strength and my mind has failed me, my heart is growing weak and all these shackles and chains around me pull me every time I run to escape,
> Jesus I am crying out to you from this deep valley.
> Suddenly I heard a voice telling me, don't give up your faith, and keep on seeking, trusting, and loving your Lord, then you'll see His glory.
> Down on my knees I prayed then I saw His grace, the Lord touched me with His grace and set me free.
> Jesus, Lord I love you.

In early 1990, my family doctor informed me that I had polycystic kidneys. I know that it's hereditary.

My mom had this disease and she died from kidney transplant failure. Now, there is a new addition to my health problem. In 2003 May, Jesus gave me a dream. In this dream, I died and it was summer. I went to my kidney specialist and asked him, "How did I die?"

He replied, "Your kidneys failed."

At the end of my dream, I was up all night and my kidneys were in massive pain. On June 1st, the Consolidated School nearby where I volunteered and worked as a teacher's assistant, held a Reunion for all those who worked there, so I went to this open house. Shortly after I arrived, I started to get this sharp pain in my kidneys again, this time I could barely walk, so I asked a parent if she mind taking me to the emergency, to the near hospital, she gladly did, and I left my car by the cemetery across from the school. At two in the morning I woke up in the emergency room, I started to get ready to go home since there was so pain within my kidneys anymore,

As I was getting ready the emergency nurse said to me, "You can't go anywhere you need to stay here till morning for your doctor to see you."

I said to her, "Why, what's wrong with me?"

She replied, "Both your kidneys have failed." I was shocked at what she said to me and the dream I had in May. I told her that I still needed to leave, because I promised this police officer that, I would move my car from the cemetery property, where I left it. So they made me sign a form and I walked out of the emergency, since it was 2 in the morning I didn't want to wake up any of my friends, and since I got a ride here I didn't have any money to take a taxi.

Thank God my apartment was only six blocks away from here. As I started to walk down this quiet street, it hit me again what the nurse just told me, tears were running down my face as I was walking home and I was singing, "Jesus loves me this I know, for the Bible tells me so." There was a pickup truck pulled up next to me, a stranger wanted to give me a ride, he was slowing down right by me, I was scared for a second, as he heard me sing loudly, "Yes Jesus loves me, yes Jesus loves me" the stranger in the car took off real fast, and I jogged the rest of the way home. Next morning June 2nd ,it's summer, I went to see my kidney specialist, and as I walked in his office the first thing I asked him, "What would happen to me now that, my kidneys failed."

He said, "You will die if you don't get dialysis A.S.A.P."

I said to him "You mean in few weeks?"

He said "No. today." Wow! God always lets me know a head of time whenever anything was about to happen to me or was coming my way. All the trials that He allowed to come my way, He always gave me a warning either by dream, vision or by speaking to me. In 2009, I ended up in an emergency, and then in intensive care, and my kidney specialist Dr. Broski told me I would die this weekend when I was in intensive care if I didn't receive a line in my body to get hemo dialysis.

As of now, I have been doing home dialysis since June 2003. I took his advice and had the surgery and went on hemo dialysis. In 2010 I almost died, every time I get a catheter to be on dialysis, the line stops working within few months, and they give me a new line till that stops then again I get a new line. God has a purpose for my life that's why I am alive today. In 2011, I had four surgeries in four days.

The surgery I had on the fourth day which was Sunday, the young surgeon came to my bedside and as he was crying, he apologized to me saying, "Shadhona I tried everything. I can't save you sorry I am so sorry." Then he walked away.

I was so sedated I wasn't able to say anything back to him I so desperately wanted to say, "Doctor please don't feel sorry for me, if I die I will be with Jesus, and if I live I will still be with my loved ones." I thought myself God always has the final say He decides if I die or live.

Living in the Valley

I woke up in the morning with line behind my ear, and it already stopped working. So now they sent me to an out-of-town hospital, an hour from here. This is all this hospital can do for me. My doctor sent me there to get an x-ray of my chest, to see if there is any possibility for a new line on my chest. After a thorough exam, the doctors almost gave up when suddenly they saw a vain on my right side of my chest and even though this doctor didn't have the authority he went ahead and did the procedure anyways. I am still alive and I had fifteen dialysis lines on my body, I can truly say that, I have been stabbed."

Pastor Henry Wiebe, my mentor says, "You are God's miracle."

Even though loving and serving God on the mountain was very exciting and so much happier ride, going to L.A. with David Wilkerson for two weeks witnessing was so full filling and satisfying, to see people accepting Jesus as their Savior, and the joy of living in Riverside California, for five months and graduating from the bible school was so thrilling, I have learned to love and trust God from the valley over these long eleven years, with my life, in the valley. I go for dialysis at the hospital three times a week, and nurses there see me as a Miracle. They were sure that, I was dying in 2011. I was supposed to live only seven days I received my catheter on the sixth day. I depend on Jesus to be alive every day. I depend on Him for everything from the day starts to the time I go to bed. There is so many complications that can go wrong for a dialysis patient, so far I had very few problems. I know of few other dialysis patients who had similar problem with their treatment and they died, here I am by His Grace still alive. I am very grateful to my Lord Jesus.

I have come to realize, it is not important where you are, but, who you are with. Any place can be a paradise if you are with the right person. I have seen couples go away to Caribbean Island to find that paradise romance, but come back miserable. When you are with the right person, you can simply be in an ordinary place, and be the happiest and feel like you are in a paradise.

Shadhona

CHAPTER 22

Lessons learned from my journey as a Christian

My life hasn't changed much. I still do dialysis for three days a week and I live an ordinary life. I volunteer at my church, which I love to do. I still feel like my life is still in the valley in some small ways. While in is this valley of living with health problem, spiritual dryness, as if it couldn't get any worse, in 2013 I experienced the worse kind of betrayal and rejection from my personal relationship and the only family I had for the past ten years. I have loved this family with Godly and unconditional love of God. It came like a shock overnight. On one Thursday my friend asked me, "How did your dialysis go?" I was driving to go to my life group after dialysis.

I was so happy that she called me. I answered, "Not good, with all the afflictions these people are afflicting me with, is taking a toll on me. I am still standing on my feet because you are standing by me. Next morning I received an e-mail from a stranger telling me to leave my friends /family alone, I felt like I was in the twilight zone; couldn't wrap my head around it. It is how she went about ending the relationship hurts me deeply. At this point, I lost my strength to fight anymore and emotionally collapsed specially when I lost my long-time friend and my family, that's the moment I collapsed both physically and emotionally. God in His mercy surrounded me with, friends who prayed for me and with me. When I collapsed, a good Samaritan name Karlene, whom I will be forever grateful to, stopped and picked me up. She cared for me through her compassion, kindness, words of wisdom, and even praying with me at times when I needed it. I am very grateful to my friend Ingrid who showed me compassion in prayer and comforting from this affliction I was going through.

Jesus always went ahead of me and prepared people in place to help me in time of need. Before this affliction even came my way, God warned me through a vision that, Three people would hurt me and turn against me, I refused and shrugged off from believing that, one of them would be my best friend, who is like a family to me, but it came true. As I look back in this journey of mine, I see how much I have learned from God, how much I have matured spiritually. Going through this valley, taught me to depend on Jesus more, trust Him more and lean on Him more. Now I am living the advice I gave my friends. I often tell them, if you ever fall into a pit of life, don't try to fight to get out on your own strength, instead ask God what he wants you to learn from this experience, and stay till God delivers you from this trial. Now when the storm comes my way I don't run against it, instead I go through it, knowing that Jesus is with me. When the darkness surrounds me, I don't dwell in this darkness that is around me; I remember God is light.

When I am weak I tell myself that Jesus is strong. Going through the valley, at times even coming close to death has helped me to build my faith muscle even stronger. Looking back in the days when, I first became a Born Again Christian, I realize how naive I was, thinking Christians are the good and safe people to be around; they are kind loving and quick to forgive. Today in my spiritual maturity and what my trials and test of time have shown me things are quite contrary to my innocent belief. I have seen some cruel, mean, vicious and malicious and unkind people who are Christians, of whom I have personally suffered from their hands. So I have learned that, the difference between a Christian and the one who is not, the Christian person has asked for God's forgiveness and accepted Jesus as her Savior and the other person did not ask for God's forgiveness, and God's gift to us His grace through Jesus.

I have also learned that Christians are not perfect; they are forgiven. As my friend Mitch would say to me "Christians are broken people. We come to church, which is a spiritual hospital, so we can heal and mend our broken heart and be more like Jesus." Today what is more important to me is that, Jesus loves me, and cares for me and He will not allow any un pleasant things to come my way, unless He sees that it would help me only to grow and mature in my walk with Him. After studying the Bible, experiencing both the walk on the mountain top with Jesus and going through the valley with Him, after witnessing to many people and watching them come to Christ.

I have learned to keep my eyes on Jesus no matter how many times I fall; to get up and brush the dirt off of my knees and continue to run gazing my eyes on Jesus. So when the strong winds blows my way I will run through it, not fight against it, because I know Jesus is right here beside me.

In Closing

I would like to leave one my most favourite recipes for my readers and my friends. As you all know I don't cook with recipes, so I will talk you through it.

Chicken Kebab

Directions

1. Cut ito small cubes two boneless and skinless chicken. In a bowl mix meat with plain yogurt and marinade for 20 minutes.
2. Take meat out into another bowl. Mix in two tablespoons of fresh ginger paste, or powder and 1 tea spoon of garlic minced.
3. Add 2 tablespoons paprika. Salt and pepper to taste. Soak bamboo skewers in cold water for 20 minutes. Mix all these ingredients well with the meat.
4. Heat a non-stick frying pan to medium high. Add 4 tablespoons spoon of canola, or vegetable oil when you see a bit of smoke on the pan.
5. Put the skewered meat in pan, after three minutes, turn them over to the other side and put pan in the oven 400 degrees for 5 more minutes and the meat should be tender and juicy.
6. For side dishes, cook jasmine-scented rice. It goes really well with the chicken kebab.
7. In a saucepan, bring 2 cups of cold water to a boil, add 1 teaspoon of cooking oil and add 1 cup of jasmine rice rinse the rice in cold water before.
8. Once the rice comes to a boil cover with lid and turn the heat to simmer on the lowest temperature on your stove. Cook the rice for 15 minutes. Fresh salsa is a delicious side also.
9. Thinly sliced cucumber, and tomato and red or sweet onion mix it well with lime juice and salt and pepper, and if you like cilantro add a few chopped cilantro. Voila, dinner is ready.

THE END.

www.ingramcontent.com/pod-product-compliance
Ingram Content Group UK Ltd.
Pitfield, Milton Keynes, MK11 3LW, UK
UKHW022216230426
12048UKWH00016BA/885